THOMAS HART BENTON: A Personal Commemorative

CENTENNIAL EDITION

THOMAS HART BENTON:
A Personal Commemorative

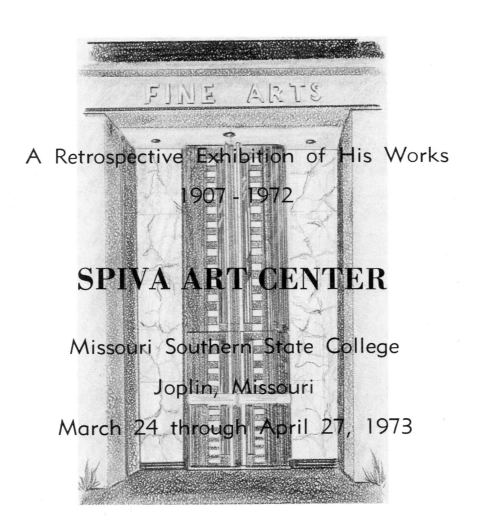

A Retrospective Exhibition of His Works

1907 - 1972

SPIVA ART CENTER

Missouri Southern State College

Joplin, Missouri

March 24 through April 27, 1973

In Honor Of The Joplin Centennial

ABOUT THE EDITOR:

Mary Curtis Warten is a native of Joplin, Missouri, who brings to this project a professional background in radio, public relations and promotion in metropolitan areas of the East, South and Midwest.

Since her marriage to Joplin attorney Henry Warten, she has been a full-time volunteer in the arts. She is president of the Joplin Council for the Arts, vice chairman of the Joplin Centennial Commission, chairman of the exhibits committee of the Spiva Art Center, and chairman of cultural affairs for the Joplin Chamber of Commerce.

She spearheaded the fund raising for the Benton mural and the exhibition, planned and organized the Thomas Hart Benton Retrospective Exhibition, and researched, compiled and edited this book.

THE CONSULTANT FOR THE EXHIBITION:

Sidney Larson is director of the art department at Columbia College, and curator of the gallery of the State Historical Society of Missouri at Columbia. A long-time friend of Thomas Hart Benton and a painter, sculptor and muralist in his own right, he has worked on restoring the Benton murals in the Missouri State Capitol at Jefferson City, and is a conservator of public and private works of art.

Mr. Larson was an assistant to Benton in the execution of the mural in the Harry S. Truman Library at Independence, Missouri. He was co-ordinator of cultural exhibits of the Missouri Pavilion of the 1964 New York World's Fair, and is listed in Who's Who in American Art. Mr. Larson has designed the placement of Benton works on exhibit at the Spiva Art Center with the assistance of Darral A. Dishman, gallery director, and his staff.

The mural was made possible in part through a matching grant from the National Endowment for the Arts, a federal agency, under its program of Works of Art in Public Places.

The Thomas Hart Benton Retrospective Exhibition was supported by a matching grant from the National Endowment for the Arts under its Museum Program of Aid to Special Exhibitions.

The book received financial assistance from the Missouri State Council on the Arts, St. Louis, Missouri, among whose officers are: Lyman Field, chairman; Mrs. Marshall Craig, vice chairman; David Morton, chairman of the visual arts committee; Frances Poteet, executive director; Joseph Fischer, curator.

PUBLISHER
BURD + FLETCHER
KANSAS CITY, MISSOURI

CONTENTS

INDEX OF ILLUSTRATIONS

WORKS

PHOTOGRAPHS

All photographic studies of Thomas Hart Benton in this book have been contributed by Karl Lee of KODE-TV and Joe Sullens of the Joplin Globe, and are reproduced with their permission.

Photographs of early Joplin are from the Joplin Mineral Museum and the historical files of the late Dorothea B. Hoover.

LENDERS TO THE EXHIBITION

Mrs. Jessie Benton, Los Angeles, California

Mr. Thomas Hart Benton, Kansas City, Missouri

Mrs. Thomas Hart Benton, Kansas City, Missouri

Mr. Thomas P. Benton, Gay Head, Massachusetts

Mr. and Mrs. John Callison, Kansas City, Missouri

Master Anthony Benton Gude, Los Angeles, California

The Metropolitan Museum of Art, New York City

Museum of Art and Archeology, University of Missouri-Columbia

Mr. and Mrs. William F. Navran, Shawnee Mission, Kansas

The Nelson Gallery-Atkins Museum, Kansas City, Missouri

Mr. Eddie Samoa, Boston, Massachusetts

The School of the Art Institute of Chicago

Mr. and Mrs. Louis Sosland, Shawnee Mission, Kansas

The State Historical Society of Missouri, Columbia

Mr. Rolla E. Stephens, Joplin, Missouri

Mr. and Mrs. Robert E. Stroud, Shawnee Mission, Kansas

Mr. and Mrs. Henry Warten, Joplin, Missouri

Mr. and Mrs. Merle E. Welsh, Prairie Village, Kansas

Mr. and Mrs. John Jefferson Wood, Overland Park, Kansas

BENEFACTORS*

Blanchard, Van Fleet, Robertson & Dermott

City of Joplin

Commerce Bank of Joplin

Mr. and Mrs. Jerry D. Connor

Mr. and Mrs. John M. Cragin

Mr. and Mrs. Robert E. Fay

First National Bank and Trust Company of Joplin

The Friends of St. Avips

The Guengerichs

Freeman Johnson Trust

Joplin Beer Wholesalers

Joplin Board of Realtors

Joplin Chamber of Commerce

The Joplin Council for the Arts

The Joplin Globe Publishing Company

Joplin Historical Society

Joplin Supply Company

The Kassab Family

Mr. Rufus Crosby Kemper

Mr. and Mrs. Carroll A. Knost

Mrs. Thornton C. Land

Mr. and Mrs. Stanford Leffen

Mr. and Mrs. Addison E. McMechan

Missouri State Council on the Arts

National Endowment for the Arts

Northpark Mall

Ruby B. Ott, In memory of Mr. and Mrs. Harry E. Blaine

Mr. and Mrs. William C. Putnam

Mr. and Mrs. William Landreth Rainey

Roberts & Fleischaker

The Grandchildren of Harrison Lang Rogers

Mr. and Mrs. Harry A. Satterlee

Judge and Mrs. Robert E. Seiler

Southwestern Bell Telephone Company

Spiva Art Center, Inc.

Mrs. George A. Spiva

The Family of Dan L. Stanley

Mr. Rolla E. Stephens

Students of the Joplin Public Schools

Mr. and Mrs. Charles L. Sweatt

United Missouri Bank of Joplin, n. a.

Mr. and Mrs. Henry Warten

Mr. Verne Wilder

*Contributors of $500 or more to the Joplin Council for the Arts - Benton Fund

To the City of Joplin
1973
Thomas H. Benton

PREFACE

Only once in a hundred years could a book like this come about.

As Joplin celebrates the opening of its Centennial March 24, 1973, it honors—and is honored by—a great American artist whose life and works span the major part of that century.

Because Thomas Hart Benton began his professional career in Joplin, he agreed, in 1971 at the age of 82, to paint a mural for the city's Municipal Building, and to lend a group of Benton works from his and his family's private collections as the nucleus of a retrospective exhibition. In two years of planning, the exhibition, appropriately entitled, "THOMAS HART BENTON: A Personal Commemorative," has become the largest and most diverse showing of Benton works to date.

This book, also, is a personal commemorative—in pictures and words. It is a catalogue of the exhibition and an account of the evolution of the mural, "JOPLIN AT THE TURN OF THE CENTURY, 1896-1906." An essay by Benton introduces the mural; another essay introduces the paintings in the show, reaffirming his philosophy of art.

In 1906, Joplin was young Tom Benton's kind of town, burgeoning with people and opportunity. The description of his summer as cartoonist on the Joplin American from his autobiography, "An Artist in America," is reprinted in this book with pertinent illustrations taken from the Joplin exhibition. In the mural, he recreates in new dimensions scenes of his memory of Joplin at the turn of the century that suggest the contradictions inherited from a rough mining camp named after a Methodist home missionary which, in its early years of city status, became for a while a lead and zinc capital of the world.

It was our idea, not Benton's, that he should paint himself into the mural. It was to be a personal remembrance of the city in which he started his art career. He pondered whether to depict himself as an old man in the midst of his memories, or in period as the 17-year old cartoonist. He offered us a choice, but made his own decision.

Another alternative was presented with his first preliminary drawing of the theme of the mural. The committee could choose a scene featuring either a real estate office or the House of Lords saloon. We unanimously settled on the latter. Every town had a real estate office, but only Joplin could boast the famous House of Lords where Benton was taunted into becoming an artist. The rejected alternative is pictured on the copyright page of this book.

In his letter accompanying the first preliminary drawing, Benton wrote: "I am still open to suggestions for the whole thematic concept. But make them NOW. Once I start work on organizing the mural, nobody can say anything that will be listened to. Remember, we sign our contract on the theme—NOT ON HOW I HANDLE IT."

Benton had no interference in his work from his Joplin sponsors, only cooperation when he asked for it. Painting the mural turned out to be an exhilarating experience for him. Friends remarked that he seemed ten years younger as he plunged into the assignment. His murals are Benton's greatest achievements, and, as he describes the process in "An Artist in America," they are "a kind of an emotional spree."

He continues, "The very thought of the large spaces puts me in an exalted frame of mind, strings up my energies, and heightens the color of the world. After I have gone through with my practical preparations, which are elaborate and occupy the major part of the time spent on any job, a certain kind of thoughtless freedom comes over me. . . . I paint with downright sensual pleasure."

The artist agreed to permit us to exhibit for the first time in a major show the clay models in diorama, which are a unique and important step in the production of all his paintings, whether for a mural or an easel picture. It is a process that he revived after much research and study of the Renaissance masters and their techniques. In his professional and technical autobiography, "An American in Art," Benton regards the tiny sculptures as "a relief map . . . and not as aesthetic products in themselves." In modeling the little figures, he purposely distorts their planes in order to accentuate the light and shade of their projections and to gain three-dimensional effects. He tilts their background at almost a forty-five degree angle. If the forward figures were to stand upright, they would appear to be falling off the finished mural.

Ordinarily, Benton destroys his clay models as soon as they have served their purpose in his compositional process. We persuaded him, however, to preserve them for our exhibition as part of its educational aspects. He reinforced them with wax and armatures for that purpose, but warned that they will disintegrate in time without careful protection.

The bronze sculptures in the show also are being exhibited for the first time in a Benton retrospective exhibition. The football figures reflect Tom Benton's enthusiasm for the sport in which he won a letter during his brief period at Western Military Academy at Alton, Illinois, before he entered the School of the Art Institute of Chicago. His sculptured players were inspired by similar figure compositions on ancient Etruscan funeral urns.

Many of the paintings in the Spiva Art Center show are being exhibited publicly for the first time, especially the Benton family portraits. The story of the discovery of Benton's lost self portrait of 1909, painted in Paris, is first published in these pages.

Most of the drawings have not been displayed before or reproduced. As working drawings, some of them bear the blemishes of their studio use, even in print. Those that trace the development of the mural are on display in the City Council Chamber of the Municipal Building, where they can be seen in connection with the mural.

The earliest known drawing to survive from Benton's student days at the Art Institute of Chicago had been preserved in Joplin by a former classmate at the Art Institute and subsequently has been authenticated by Benton for this exhibition. Two other drawings of 1907-08 are shown through the courtesy of the School of the Art Institute of Chicago, where they were rediscovered recently in a scrapbook and lent to Rutgers University for a 1972 retrospective exhibition of Benton's early years, 1907-1929.

The full impact of any work of art cannot be realized in reproduction. Reducing it to the size of a printed page and substituting ink for paint diminishes its force and disturbs the subtle orchestrations of its colors. For hundreds of visitors to the Spiva Art Center and the Joplin Municipal Building, this will be their first experience with original major works of art.

Furthermore, works that exist in separate locations give only fragmentary glimpses of an artist and his development. The exhibit, "THOMAS HART BENTON: A Personal Commemorative," has been assembled in an effort to present the whole man in perspective through varied and representative works of all the periods of his long and distinguished career which began in Joplin. Only space has limited the number of paintings we might have shown.

The works exhibited here are to be shared as an extraordinary birthday tribute to the City of Joplin and to the people of his home country by Thomas Hart Benton. This book is the permanent record of that event and of the creation of his last mural.

Mary Curtis Warten
Editor

A CHRONOLOGICAL AUTOBIOGRAPHY

THOMAS HART BENTON

1889

Born Neosho, Newton County, Missouri. Parents "Colonel" Maecenas E. and Elizabeth Wise Benton. Col. Benton served in Confederate Army and settled in Neosho as a lawyer in 1869. He became politically prominent under President Cleveland as U. S. Attorney for the Western District of Missouri, and subsequently went for five terms to the Congress of the United States.

1894-99

Began drawing Indians and railroad trains. Executed first mural with crayons on newly papered staircase wall in Benton home at Neosho. Work unappreciated. Grade schools in Washington, D. C. First introduced to formal art in the Library of Congress and the Corcoran Gallery in Washington.

1900-04

Finished grade school. Met Buffalo Bill and saw his Wild West Show. Had first training in art at Western High School in Georgetown. Visited St. Louis World's Fair. Saw first Remington pictures and shook hands with the last fighting Indian chief, Geronimo. Returned, with father's political defeat, to all-year residence in Neosho.

1905-06

High school in Neosho. Began acquiring steady reading habits in father's library and with dime novels in the hayloft. Continued drawing work in summer of 1906 as surveyor's assistant, rodman, around Joplin, Missouri, mining field. Found position as cartoonist on The Joplin American—first professional work as artist.

1906-07

Attended Western Military Academy at Alton, Illinois, until February, when serious study of art was begun at Chicago Art Institute. Abandoned plans of doing newspaper work and took up painting.

1908-11

Went to France. Enrolled at Academie Julien, Paris. Made first approach to classic composition and to anatomy and perspective. Learned French. Attended lectures and musical events. Developed life-long attachment to chamber music. Painted in various opposed manners from "Academic" chiaroscuro of Academie Julien to "Pointilist" landscape. Met with many personalities later to become famous in the art world, such as Leo Stein, brother of the famous Gertrude, John Marin, Jacob Epstein, Jo Davidson, Andre L'Hote, Leon Kroll, Diego Rivera, Morgan Russell, and Stanton McDonald Wright. Was an habitue of cafes and studios where problems of new art were vociferously discussed. Stimulated by work in galleries of the Louvre, began the study of art history. Read extensively in French literature, aesthetics, and philosophy, along with classics. Became acquainted with Balzac, Baudelaire, Verlaine, Gautier, de Musset and other writers who were in vogue at the time. Read Hippolyte Taine's "Philosophie de l'Art", whose environmental aesthetic was to have its full effect later when American "regionalism" became an issue in the art world. Influenced by Zuloaga, well known Spanish painter, and became interested in Spanish school. Out of this grew later fascination for El Greco. Left France and returned to America without any defined directions of style.

1912

Stayed a few months at hometown, Neosho, Missouri. Made an abortive effort to settle in Kansas City, then moved on to New York.

1913-16

Struggled to make a living and find a "way to painting". Occasional commercial art jobs, decorative work in over-glaze ceramics, set designing, historical reference and portrait work for the moving picture industry, then mostly located at Fort Lee, New Jersey, across the Hudson from New York. Worked with directors Rex Ingram and Gordon Edwards, and with such stars of the day as Theda Bara, Clara Kimball Young, Stuart Holmes, etc. Set up a studio in an old house at Fort Lee, and met Walt Kuhn, "Pop" Hart, Arthur B. Davies and other artists who frequented the west side of the Hudson River. Tried acting, unsuccessfully. Met Alfred Stieglitz and frequented his gallery at 291 Fifth Avenue. Intimates of the period: Rex Ingram, the movie director; Thomas Craven, then a poet and teacher; Willard Huntington Wright, art critic and editor of "Smart Set," known later as S. S. Van Dine of detective story fame; Ralph Barton, famous caricaturist; and Stanton McDonald Wright, earlier friend who had returned from Paris, a city now war-ridden. In spring of 1916, had first public exhibition with a series of paintings in the Forum Exhibition of Modern American Painting held at Anderson Galleries in New York. These paintings, though mostly "figurative," were variants of the synchromist "form through color" practices of Morgan Russell and S. McDonald Wright. They were highly generalized, purely compositional, and contained no hint of the environmentalist work of later years. Began to sell an occasional picture. Joined "People's Art Guild," dominated by socialist theory and founded by Dr. John Weischel, a mathematician, social theorist and critic well known in "radical" circles of New York. "The People's Art Guild" was designed to bring art to the workers and to enlist the interest of the unions. At the Friday night discussions of the Guild was introduced to the thinking of Owen, Prud'hon and Marx. Ideas about the social meanings and values of art were germinated in these discussions. They were to bear fruit later. Met Bob Minor, Max Eastman, John Sloan, Mike Gold, and the other "radical" artists of the Old Masses magazine. Entered into first controversies at Stieglitz 291 gallery on future values of "representational" versus "abstract" art. This was the beginning of a series of controversies on the purpose and meaning of art which was to last for more than thirty years. Met an extraordinary income producing patron, Dr. Alfred Raabe, who would pick up studio experiments, frame them, and sell them to his patients in the Bronx.

1917

Through "People's Art Guild" obtained position as gallery director and art teacher for "Chelsea Neighborhood Association" on the lower West Side, which was supported by well-to-do conservatives but followed the social directions of the "People's Art Guild." It had little success, but provided a skimpy living in the difficult period of America's entrance into World War I.

1918

Enlisted in the U. S. Navy. Shoveled coal for a month, engaged in Saturday night athletic exhibitions, boxing and wrestling, and ended up finally as draughtsman at Norfolk Naval Base. Sketched constantly during "off-duty" periods. Spent evenings reading American history.

1919

Returned to New York with Navy discharge and collection of drawings and watercolors of Naval Base activities. Though at times semi-abstract, this was first work based wholly on environmental observations of the American scene. It was shown at the Daniel Galleries in New York and received considerable public attention. Continued reading American history and conceived idea of a series of paintings to illustrate its progressions. This constituted a return to mid-19th century subject painting and involved a definite break with modern theory, which was moving away from representa-

tional concerns towards pure abstraction. Started tentative designs for this historical project and, to increase their objectivity, began modeling the designs in clay. This was a frank return to Renaissance method. The emphasis involved, on chiaroscuro and realistic form rather than color patterns, caused another step away from accepted modern theories.

1920-24

Continued moving toward "realistic" subject painting and present style of painting now developed, largely determined by practice of modeling compositions. Pictures began attracting considerable attention and argument. Participated in 1922 Philadelphia Exhibition of Modern Americans and sold a large work to the famous Philadelphia collector, Albert C. Barnes. Married Rita Piacenza. Began diagrammatic analysis of the compositional history of occidental painting. This project was undertaken for Albert Barnes but, because it failed to jibe with his growing "color-form" theories, it led to disagreement and was never finished. Sections of it were later published in the Arts Magazine (1926-27). Began showing series of paintings on American historical themes at the Architectural League in New York. These were mural size works. They were controversial because, with their sculptural and three-dimensional character, they were in opposition to prevalent beliefs of architects and critics that mural paintings should not break wall surfaces but remain flat and linear in the manner of the French muralist, Puvis de Chavannes. Published first theoretical paper, "Form and the Subject" in Arts Magazine, June 1924. During the period, began exploring the back countries of America by foot, bus and train, searching out American subject matter.

1925-27

Gave series of lectures on art at Dartmouth College and at Bryn Mawr College. Thomas P. Benton, first child, born in New York City in 1926. Through influence of the famous draughtsman, Boardman Robinson, obtained permanent teaching position at the Art Students League in New York, which supplied a much needed basic income. Debated with Frank Lloyd Wright on architecture and mural painting at Brown University, Providence, Rhode Island. Debate punctuated with complete disagreements on relation of architecture and painting. Purchased permanent summer home on Island of Martha's Vineyard, Massachusetts.

1928-29

Joined with Clemente Orozco, famous Mexican painter then living in New York, in exhibitions at the Delphic Galleries. Showed drawings and paintings of the current American scene, the outcome of the exploratory travels mentioned earlier. Among paintings were "Boomtown," now at Rochester Museum; "Cotton Pickers," now at Metropolitan Museum in New York; also "Rice Threshing," now at Brooklyn Museum. Received commission with Orozco to do murals for the New School for Social Research. These murals were executed for little more than expenses, but offered opportunity for a public trial of the new mural styles.

1930-31

Drawing upon mass of factual material gathered in travels, the New School mural, "Modern America," was painted. This was the first large scale American work executed with egg tempera. It was both widely praised and heavily criticized. Reproductions were published in magazines and newspapers all over the world. Through Thomas Craven, met John Steuart Curry. Because of similar beliefs and interests, an enduring tie was made with Curry. It lasted until his death.

1932

Received commission from Mrs. Juliana Force to do murals for library of Whitney Museum of American Art. Finished and unveiled in December. These murals again drew sharp criticism. Fellow instructors at the Art Students League drew up a round robin letter of condemnation. The New Republic published a special article on the mural's inadequacies. Representing facets of ordinary American life and folk lore, the Marxist group of New York attacked the work as a form of chauvinism, as politically reactionary and "isolationist." A "question-answer" appearance on the meaning of the murals at the John Reed Club, the center of artistic and literary radicalism in New York, wound up in a chair-throwing brawl and resulted in the loss of many old radical-minded friends. From this time on, "American Regionalist" works would never be free of the political charges — "reactionary" or "isolationist."

1933

Given Gold Medal of Architectural League for mural work. Received commission and executed mural for the State of Indiana. This mural, 200 feet long by 12 feet high, was researched, planned and executed in six months of intensive labor. Covering the theme of social evolution of Indiana, it was shown as Indiana's exhibit at the 1933 Chicago World's Fair. It now is installed in the University of Indiana Auditorium at Bloomington. The work was well received. Criticism was leveled chiefly at the propriety of the subject matter. The

inclusion of Indiana's Ku Klux Klan episode drew most of the objection.

1934

Received commission from Treasury Department for a mural in new Federal Post Office in Washington, D. C. Abandoned work during planning stages because of difficulties in accommodating artistic ideas to those of Treasury Art Commission. Took on a country-wide lecture tour on American Art. Speaking at Iowa University met Grant Wood, and, as with Curry, established an intimate and enduring friendship. After a lecture at Kansas City Art Institute, went with brother, Nat Benton, and State Senator Ed Barbour, to Jefferson City, where preliminary discussions about a mural for Missouri State Capitol were begun. Returning to New York, had exhibit of paintings at Ferargil Galleries along with Grant Wood and John S. Curry, and thus became permanently associated with "Regionalism" or the "Regionalist School." There was no such "school," but the designation "regionalist" stuck. Time magazine catapulted the "school" into national attention with a Benton self portrait in color on its cover and a well documented article on the "New American Art." Gave lecture to a large audience at the Art Students League Auditorium on "American Art and Social Realism." Bitter debate from the floor. This was followed by attacks in art magazines and pamphlets on "provincialism" of regionalist aesthetics.

1935

Received commission for mural in Missouri State Capitol, along with a request to head department of painting at Kansas City Art Institute. Seeing in the latter a chance to escape continuing New York controversy, promptly accepted. Moved to Kansas City. Spent the year teaching and planning Capitol mural.

1936

Executed Missouri mural. Here again, a storm of criticism arose, mostly, as in Indiana, about subject matter. Mural was given wide attention in the press. It eventually came to please, or at least interest, most Missourians, and remains on the Capitol walls.

1937-38

Wrote "Artist in America" for McBride publishing house in New York. Book autobiographical — chiefly a report on American travel. Very successful. Reported on "sit-down" strikes in Detroit for Life magazine with a series of on-the-spot sketches. Made for same magazine a painting and a forty-drawing commentary on Hollywood and the movie industry, latter not published. Made series of drawings on 1937 floods in Southeast Missouri for St. Louis Post Dispatch and Kansas City Star. Wrote and illustrated (1938) an article for Scribners magazine on Disney, Oklahoma, then on the boom. Painted "Susannah and the Elders." This once controversial nude now in Museum of the Palace of the Legion of Honor at San Francisco. Began a series of lithographs on the American scene for Associated American Artists of New York, which eventually ran to some fifty stones. Sold "Cradling Wheat" to St. Louis Art Museum.

1939

Illustrated Tom Sawyer for George Macy's "Limited Editions." Became interested in texture, an aspect of painting neglected during years predominately devoted to murals. Painted "Persephone," another highly publicized nude. Purchased present Kansas City home. Jessie P. Benton born. Had retrospective exhibition at William Rockhill Nelson Gallery in Kansas City, which went afterward to Associated American Artists' new galleries in New York. From this exhibition, Metropolitan Museum purchased its second Benton, "Roasting Ears." All except the very large works in this exhibition were sold. This was first substantial success with a New York exhibition.

1940-42

Illustrated John Steinbeck's "Grapes of Wrath" for "Limited Editions." Lecture tour, teaching experiments with texture painting and increased coloration. New interest in Flemish paintings stimulated partly by Grant Wood and partly by exhibitions of such paintings held at Nelson Gallery in Kansas City. Fired from position at Kansas City Art Institute after various disagreements with trustees. Illustrated "Huckleberry Finn" for "Limited Editions." Made an album of flute, harmonica and voice with son, Thomas P., an accomplished flutist, and Frank Luther's singers for Decca records, "Tom Benton's Saturday Night." Music based on American folk songs, especially composed for album. Was lecturing in Cincinnati, Ohio, when news of Pearl Harbor was released. Returned to Kansas City and commenced series of war paintings designed to help awaken American public to dangers of the moment. This series was purchased by Abbott Laboratories of Chicago. Reproduced in full color, it was presented in book and poster form to U. S. Government for propaganda use. Distribution of reproductions ran to 18,000,000 copies. Exhibition of original paintings at Associated American Artists in New York attracted 75,000 people. Paintings were later presented by Abbott Laboratories to Missouri Historical Society at Columbia. Painted "Negro Soldier," also now at Missouri His-

torical Society, and "Prelude to Death," World War II embarkation scene, both in present exhibition in Joplin.

1943-44

Continued paintings and drawings of the war for Abbott Laboratories and U. S. Government. Visited industrial plants, training camps, oil fields. Went to sea on submarine, and down Ohio and Mississippi and into Gulf of Mexico on L.S.T. Illustrated Mark Twain's "Life on the Mississippi" for "Limited Editions." By end of 1944, returned to normal painting activity. Wrote article on Grant Wood (now deceased) for University of Kansas City Review.

1945

Made Honorary Member of Argentine Academia Nacional de Bellas Artes. Productive year. Among paintings, "July Hay," was third to go to Metropolitan Museum. "Flood Time," now in collection of Harpo Marx, and "Custer's Last Stand," now in the Richard Russell collection, Scarsdale, New York.

1946

Exhibition of paintings at Chicago galleries of Associated American Artists. Chicago press generally receptive, although an echo of the old New York charge of "provincial" was heard. Received commission for mural at Harzfeld's store in Kansas City. Went to Hollywood and worked with Walt Disney on plans for an American operetta on the theme of "Davy Crockett." Could not accommodate to Disney needs and abandoned project.

1947

Executed Harzfeld's mural, "Achelous and Hercules." Encyclopedia Britannica made film of mural's technical progressions which had international distribution.

1948

Wrote article on John Steuart Curry, after his death, for University of Kansas City Review. Began intense study of West — New Mexico, Utah and Wyoming. These areas began taking place of Middle West and South, which had heretofore furnished bulk of "regionalist" subjects. Received honorary degree of Doctor of Arts from University of Missouri. Made honorary Phi Beta Kappa.

1949

Returned to Europe. In Italy, made honorary member of L'Accademia Fiorentina delle Arti del Disegno at Florence, and of Accademia Senese degli Intronati at Siena. Revisited Paris. Had a hard time reviving French, which now had a Missouri accent.

1951

Retrospective exhibition at Joslyn Museum, Omaha, Nebraska. Added chapter to a new edition of "Artist in America," which reawakened old New York controversies about "regionalism" in the Saturday Review of Literature.

1952-53

Revisited France and Italy. Returned to America with Admiral James Flateley on U.S.S. "Block Island." Made lithograph illustrations for University of Oklahoma Press limited editions of Lynn Riggs' "Green Grow the Lilacs." Painted Lincoln mural for Lincoln University at Jefferson City, Missouri.

1954

New York's Whitney Museum, moving to new quarters, gave its Benton murals to Museum of New Britain, Connecticut. Along with exhibition of murals, the Institute staged a retrospective showing of Benton paintings. Institute also purchased portrait of "Dennys Wortman" and portrait of "Benton" by Dennys Wortman.

1955

Made study trip to Spain. Received commission for, and began planning mural, "Old Kansas City," for Kansas City River Club.

1956

Finished River Club mural and received commission from Power Authority of the State of New York for a mural representing discovery of the St. Lawrence River by Jacques Cartier. Began research and planning for work.

1957

Executed St. Lawrence mural, now installed in New York Power Authority administration building at Massena, New York. Received honorary degree of Doctor of Letters from Lincoln University, Jefferson City, Missouri.

1958

Painted the "Sheepherder," an interpretation of the Grand Teton Mountains in Wyoming. Now divided time between home in Kansas City and summer home on Martha's Vineyard. Occasionally lectured and taught at University of Kansas City, and elsewhere. Signed a contract with the Truman Memorial Library, Independence, Missouri, for an historical mural on the theme, "Independence and the Opening of the West"; and another with the Power Authority of the State of New York for a mural on "The Discovery of Niagara Falls by Father Hennepin."

1959

Worked on plans for above murals. Researched in the field and at museums and historical societies. Found models for Pawnee and Cheyenne Indians through help of Charles Banks Wilson, Oklahoma artist, and Brummit Echo Hawk, Pawnee artist. With Wilson went along as much of Old Santa Fe Trail as could be found, to the site of Bent's Fort, and beyond to Spanish Peaks in South Colorado Rockies. For Oregon Trail section of Truman mural, was driven by Aaron Pyle, West Nebraska artist, to Chimney and Courthouse Rocks, landmarks of Oregon Trail. Books of drawings made on research trips.

1960-61

Finished mural designs. November 17, 1960, started execution of Truman mural. Installed canvas in studio seven feet by twenty feet for Niagara mural. Planned to work on this when weather was too bad to get over to the Truman Library at Independence. Finished both murals in the spring of 1961. Developed bad bursitis condition while working on Truman mural which went over whole body. Finished both murals under cortisone treatment. Dedication of Truman mural was presided over by President Truman and Chief Justice Earl Warren. It was a memorable occasion.

1962

Overcame bursitis condition and effects of cortisone. Decided, however, that I was getting too old for mural work and began thinking again in terms of easel painting. In May 1962, my hometown of Neosho gave me a "homecoming celebration." This was a delightful honor. President and Mrs. Truman went with a whole special trainload of friends from Kansas City to the celebration. Only a small handful of the friends of my youth were left in Neosho. Elected member of the National Academy of Arts and Letters.

1963

Revisited Wyoming in summer on a sketching trip. Painted a complicated composition of "The Twist" dance scene.

1964

In good physical shape again. Made interesting trip into Canadian Rockies. Rode horseback from Banff to Assineboine. Nine and a half hours of riding divided into two days. First horse ride in many years, certainly more than thirty years. Made a series of drawings of Mt. Assineboine, and, in the autumn, started a large painting from these.

1965

Finished painting of Assineboine, called "Trail Riders." Resigned from American Academy of Arts and Letters because of an inappropriate and compromising political speech by the organization's president. Went on a long exploratory expedition up the Missouri River from Omaha, Nebraska, to Three Forks, Montana, and from there into the "Rendezvous" area of the Wind River Mountains in Wyoming. Five weeks trip, following routes of Lewis and Clark and the fur traders and trappers. Went, in autumn, to Italy for two months to try hand (in American sculptor-painter Harry Jackson's Italian studio) at bronze sculpture. Learned modeling in wax. Made tour, Orvieto to Venice, across Apennines. Revisited Padova, Bologna, Florence, etc.

1966

Mr. Lyle Woodcock, St. Louis collector, set up exhibition of Benton paintings, drawings and lithographs at Illinois College, Jacksonville, Illinois. Well received. Had "stroke," followed by heart attack. Remained in hospital five weeks. Recovered, but mode of life would have to change. Now among the "old folks." Large retrospective in Detroit, Michigan, in October. Reelected to American Academy of Arts and Letters under sponsorship of Alan Nevins, American historian and new president of Academy.

1967

Selected group of representative drawings for publication by University of Missouri Press. Wrote a new chapter for "An Artist in America" for a third edition of the book, also to be published by University of Missouri Press.

1968

Above books published. Wrote "An American in Art," a technical review of my career, for The University Press of Kansas. Collaborated with Creekmore Fath, of Austin, Texas, on a book covering lithographic work.

1969

"An American in Art" published by The University Press of Kansas. "Benton Lithographs," edited by Creekmore Fath, published by University of Texas Press.

1970

Painting continued as it had always. Executed self portrait, with hands, showing old man getting older but still going. Made new lithograph of portrait. Sculpture, with five figures, of football subject was put underway.

1971

Made frontal self portrait lithograph for a new book, publisher Harry Abrams, New York City, which will cover full career. Football sculpture cast in bronze. Commission offered, and accepted, for mural celebrating 100th anniversary of the incorporation of the City of Joplin, Missouri.

1972

Completed Joplin mural in April. Spent four months of the summer building a stone retaining wall to control erosion on our beach at Martha's Vineyard. The wall is sixty feet long, from four to seven feet thick, and in some places twelve feet high. For moving the larger stones I had the help of younger men, John, Dick, Mark and Eddie, but I did most of the work myself. If the wall stands up to its purpose, I shall have defeated one of the forces of nature and thus arrived at my greatest achievement. Immediate side achievement—lost pot belly.

1973

Came to Joplin for its Centennial celebration and the unveiling of the mural.

1975
Died

THE JOPLIN PERIOD

From the Autobiography
"An Artist in America"
By Thomas Hart Benton

AMONG the odd jobs I had had around home was one with a surveying party who were laying out our waterworks system. I carried the rod and chain. A cousin of mine was a surveyor up in the lead-and-zinc country to the north, near Joplin, the big town of our world. I wrote him for work and on the basis of my little experience he gave me a job. We worked around in the burning sun of the diggings, over shale and crushed rock which shimmered in the heat and burned through the leather of our boots. Lead and zinc were on the rise at this time and Joplin, the center of the industry, was on the boom. It was a lively town, full of people. The saloon doors—and there were plenty of them—swung constantly. Money was being made, and all the devices of our rough-and-ready civilization were set up to see that it was spent. Everything was there—drugstores, slot machines, real-estate slickers, soliciting preachers, and off the main street, a row of houses devoted to insinuatingly decorated girls. On Saturday nights I went into town and looked things over. There were friends of the family in Joplin, respectable people, but I steered clear of them. I'd left home mainly to get away from contact with respectability. I was in an independent frame of mind. No one questioned my grown-up status. I went in the saloons, drank beer, and put nickels in the slot machines, I was really a man, seventeen years old now, and foot-loose.

One Saturday night I went to town and into the "House of Lords," Joplin's main saloon. I had kept out of there because I knew it was the gathering place not only for miners and entertaining roughnecks but for the substantial businessmen of the whole region, and I didn't want to risk meeting anyone who would know me and make me come out to some family dinner where I'd get treated as a boy and where my consequence would depend wholly on the fact that I was Colonel M. E.'s son. But the House of Lords had a big name for glittering swank and I had to see it. I went in and ordered a beer. Across from the bar hung a big painting. This was a famous painting in the locality. It depicted a naked girl with a mask on her face. She was lying across a sort of bed and appeared to be dying from a knife wound. In the background was a young man in fancy costume. He was about to stab himself. I believe that the story, which hung in gold letters beside the picture, told that the girl was his sister with whom, after a night at a masked ball, he had engaged in amorous play, ignorant of the relationship that existed between them. In any case, it was someone he shouldn't have been playing with in the nude, so he had stuck his knife into her and was ready to go to work on himself. I must have got sufficiently absorbed in this masterpiece to attract attention, for I became aware of some laughing down the bar, and I turned around to meet a line of grinning fellows and a barrage of kidding. These fellows saw how young I was. They probably sensed how hard I was laboring to be a man and they laid into me with all the obscenities bearing on the picture they could think of. They made me hot with embarrassment. In desperate defense of my position, I stated that I wasn't particularly interested in the naked girl but that I was studying the picture because I was an artist and wanted to see how it was done.

"So, you're an artist, Shorty?" one of my tormentors asked skeptically.

"Yes, by God! I am." I said. "And I'm a good one."

YOUNG TOM BENTON AT THE HOUSE OF LORDS IN JOPLIN, MISSOURI, 1906
1971, Oil Sketch, 16 x 25''
Collection of the Artist

Early in the summer of 1971, in his studio at Martha's Vineyard, Benton attempted to evoke on canvas the scene at the House of Lords that had sparked his career in art. Regarding it merely as an exercise in nostalgia, he abandoned the quickly executed oil sketch as an unsuitable subject to be included in the Joplin mural, even if he should decide to accept the commission. The picture still is unfinished.

The original painting that had hung behind the bar of the House of Lords has not been located since it was removed from the saloon during the prohibition era. In recreating from memory "The Brother's Remorse," Benton slightly altered the death scene. He froze the action at the moment just before the man stabbed his sister, confessing that he couldn't bear to paint a dying woman.

I don't really remember the conversation that followed, but those kidding roughnecks with their good-humored, amused faces, lost as they are to me in the vague memory of the shining bar at the House of Lords, with its bright lights, glittering silver and glassware, determined in a way the life I was to follow. Their bantering skepticism about my claims of artistry tied together the loose strings of all the purposeless activities of my adolescence. They threw me back on the only abilities that distinguished me from the run of boys, those abilities which I had abandoned for more active things. By a little quirk of fate, they made a professional artist of me in a short half-hour. One of them asked me where I was working. When I declared that I was out of a job but looking for one, he suggested that I should try the newspaper and, probably to test the veracity of my artistic claims, even offered to take me there. There was nothing for me to do but to accept. So I was led down the next block where some brightly lit second-floor windows shone above a dark stairway which tunneled steeply up to them. I went up. And I went, strangely enough, with perfect confidence.

I don't think that it had ever seriously occurred to me before that I wanted to be an artist. Certainly, until the kidding in the House of Lords, I had never declared myself one. I had never thought of being an artist in any definite way. In school and at home I gave lip service to the idea, because the practice of drawing, besides giving me pleasure, allowed me to avoid boresome study hours. But I would never take any training. I didn't see my drawing critically as something to improve but merely as a means of describing things that interested me. After I made a picture, I cared nothing for what happened to it. When I entered the stairway leading up to the Joplin American, I hadn't touched a pencil for many months. Yet I was as sure of myself as if I were a trained and constant practitioner.

At the top of the stairs I came into a long room smelling of printer's ink, hot iron, and oil. In the front was a desk where a man with a short gray beard sat reading. He was alone.

"Do you need an artist on this paper?" I asked.

He looked up at me and smiled. He had a kindly face. After a little while, with an amused chuckle, he replied, "Yes, we need an artist," and then as I stood silent, "but we need a good one."

"I'm your man," I said, and believed it.

"Are you?" he laughed.

We were silent for a while. Then after a bit of rumination, he led me to the front window. "Sonny, do you see that drugstore across the street?"

"Yes."

"Do you see that man behind the counter near the window?"

"Yes."

"Well, go over there. Tell him you're the artist from the American and that you want to make a sketch of him. Make it look like him. I don't know whether we can use you or not, but if you can make a drawing that'll look like that man there's a pretty fair chance we can give you work."

Borrowing a pencil and sheet of paper, I made my sketch— the first that I'd ever made directly from a living person. It was, by the grace of God, a sort of likeness. I took it back to the newspaper office. There were several men there now and they passed my sketch around. "Can you do that in ink?" someone asked.

"Yes," I said, "I can. I've done a lot of pictures in pen and ink."

I got the job. Fourteen dollars a week! This was monumental as compared with the four dollars I was making by carrying the rod over the hot rock of the diggings. I bade my cousin and the surveying outfit good-by and rented a room in Joplin.

Pretty soon I teamed up with the paper's cub reporter, now Ben Reese of the St. Louis Post Dispatch, and settled down to a newspaperman's life. I learned the jargon of the press and inked my drawings under the red-hot corrugated iron roof of the office. It was my business to draw some prominent person of the town each day. The heads of my drawings I made big and set them on little bodies, according to the cartoon fashion of the day. Around my people I drew the paraphernalia of their trade or business. Somebody at the office supplied the comment. This was a feature designed to interest the town in the new paper. How I did the work is a mystery to me. How I made my heads recognizable as individuals is beyond explanation. I would start with the nose and hang the other features on to it, but somehow or other, in this crazy way, I managed to make likenesses.

All summer I worked for the American. In the afternoons I clamped my foot importantly on the bar rail of the House of Lords and drank beer with the miners, the mine owners, the businessmen, and the newspapermen. Everything was jake. I was a man—and free. I was completely satisfied, except when I caught sight of my face in the mirror of the bar. It annoyed me that I looked so young.

I made the acquaintance of a fellow who frequented the houses of the decorated girls. He took me with him occasionally and I sat in the parlor and drank beer at a dollar a bottle. One night my virginity was taken by a black-haired young slut who wore a flaming red kimono and did her hair in curls like a little girl. The experience clashed with my submerged romanticism and I looked no further into the mysteries of sex.

One day, toward autumn, I went home for a week end. My family were very uneasy about my staying in Joplin. They were not sure but that the town offered too many opportunities for a seventeen-year-old boy to go to hell. Besides, they were worried about my education. They wanted me to finish high school and go to college. Having tasted freedom, academic harness was abhorrent to me, and I balked. What! Another year of high school and then four years more? Unthinkable! I was a man of the world, and no damned schoolboy. If I quit the paper, I wanted to go to Chicago and study art. I knew there was a big art school in Chicago. I'd study there for a year and then get a big-time newspaper job and get rich. The family objected to this and after hours of discussion we reached a compromise. I agreed to do a year in a military school up in Alton, Illinois, if I could go to Chicago the next. I gave up my job on the Joplin American and found myself strutting around in a gray uniform. I couldn't smoke in the military school so I chewed tobacco. I went out for the football team and got my letter. When the football season ended the place was a bore to me. I couldn't stand it.

The beginning of the year saw me in Chicago. I rode in an automobile from the railroad station to my first room in a big city. I had seen a few automobiles in Joplin, but I had never been in one. In Chicago there was horse manure on the streets, but the smell of gas was beginning to dominate its rich aroma.

The century's corner was turned.

SELF PORTRAIT IN CARICATURE, 1907-08
Pen and Ink, 6¼ x 3"
From the Stadeker Scrapbook
Collection of The School of The Art Institute of Chicago
Courtesy of The Art Institute of Chicago

SELF PORTRAIT SKETCH, 1907-08
Pen and Ink, 4¾ x 3¾"
From the Stadeker Scrapbook
Collection of The School of The Art Institute of Chicago
Courtesy of The Art Institute of Chicago

Tom Benton was proficient in drawing long before he was introduced to the pleasures of painting at the Art Institute of Chicago. Boyhood contemporaries in Neosho recall his pictures of Indians scrawled over everything from drugstore placards to berry sheds. During his father's Congressional years in Washington, D. C., young Tom filled notebooks and tablets with drawings of bloody battles from history. On his own, he had picked up a crosshatching style from John Berryman, cartoonist for the Washington Post, which was to serve him well on his first job with the Joplin American.

Under the guidance of Frederick Oswald, his favorite teacher at The School of the Art Institute of Chicago, Benton developed his first insights into composing pictures before he began them. Whistler's work appealed greatly to the young artist, as did the undulating curves and patterns of Japanese prints, which were just beginning to make their impact on the Western world.

It was in the manner of Whistler that Benton executed the Self Portrait Sketch shown here. It was rediscovered recently in the scrapbook of Claire Stadeker, a classmate at the Institute.

The lower drawing was preserved by another classmate of his Chicago days, the former Myrtle Irwin of Carthage, Missouri, who became Mrs. Clarence Craig of Joplin. Now in the possession of Mrs. Craig's granddaughter, it has been identified by Benton as a class exercise in the style of Daniel Vierge, a popular Spanish illustrator of that time. His handwritten comments appear below.

This drawing, somewhat in imitation of the style of Daniel Vierge, a Spanish pen & ink artist famous at the time (1907), was made during my first year at the Chicago Art Institute. It was done in the class of an instructor named Peixotto. (Hence the pencil signature) & I doubt if any like it survive because a fire in the family home at Neosho, MO. destroyed nearly all youthful work —

Thomas W. Benton

CLASSROOM DRAWING UNDER THE INSTRUCTION OF PEIXOTTO, 1907
The School of the Art Institute of Chicago
Pen and Ink, 11¾ x 8¾"
Collection of Mr. and Mrs. John Jefferson Wood, Overland Park, Kansas

THE JOPLIN MURAL

The

KODE-TV Photographs by Karl Lee

THE MURAL

IN 1961, when I finished the mural for the Truman Library at Independence, Mo., I said that I would not do any more large scale painting. I figured I was getting too old to go on climbing up and down ladders. And I was. So, when it was proposed, in 1971, that I do a mural for the City of Joplin to help celebrate the one hundredth anniversary of its incorporation, I didn't take much to the idea. What had tired me out in 1961 would tire me more in 1971 or '72.

But the Joplin folks interested in the mural had some persuaders. They reminded me that I had started my artistic career in Joplin when, back in 1906, I had worked there as a cartoonist on a newspaper, and they said it would be a wonderful thing to round out that career by coming back to where it had begun with a painting which showed how things looked then. All it seemed necessary to do was jog my memory and paint the Joplin I knew as a boy.

Now the Joplin I knew as a boy was a pretty engaging place. It was just becoming a city and was full of boisterous energy and all kinds of vigorous American hoopla. It was also the first place where I got free of parental supervision, where I could freely experiment with the various ways in which boys are supposed to turn themselves into men, always a fascinating occupation and one which generally leaves quite lasting impressions. So I got sort of interested in what my Joplin friends were proposing.

Every old codger likes, now and then, to recall his youth and, if he can get anybody to pay attention, tell stories about it. Here an opportunity was offered to tell some of mine and in a way that would almost compel attention. Added to this tempting prospect was the fact that the mural would not be tall enough to make ladder climbing necessary, and the further fact that it could be executed in my own studio. Weighing all this, I finally decided I wasn't too old to take on the job.

I am glad I made that decision. I got some real kicks out of the work. I got a pretty good one when I discovered I could handle the physical side of it, stand up to it six or seven hours a day, just about as easily as when I was twenty years younger. But the greatest kicks came from telling my stories, from creating and putting together a bunch of images that would look like what I remembered about 1906 Joplin.

More often than not, things we seem to remember quite vividly turn out to be only vaguely remembered when we try to describe them precisely. Generally, we satisfy ourselves by stringing a few words together which, if they seem plausible, and flattering enough to ourselves, we substitute for the real things remembered. But this doesn't work so well when visual facts are involved, because other people remember such facts too and will quickly find the errors of any visual substitutes you put forward, especially if they themselves cherish some, perhaps unconsciously made, substitutes of their own. The pulchritude of boyhood sweethearts depends on who is remembering them, whether they are yours or somebody else's. So I knew I had to be pretty accurate with my representations.

I arrived at a workable theme for the mural, a paintable theme, almost immediately after I started thinking about it. As had been suggested, I would show the young booming city of Joplin, but I would also try to show what made it boom. This seemed easy enough because I had known both. I had worked for a while as a surveyor's assistant, carrying the rod and chain, among the innumerable miners' diggings which surrounded the city before I got my job there as cartoonist. So there was no problem about what I was going to paint. But there soon arose a considerable one when the question of how began to come up, because there I ran into the above mentioned imprecision of memory.

Fortunately, my Joplin friends were able to dig up some old photographs which showed the physical aspects of both the city and the diggings as these were around the time I worked there. They were of incalculable help in sharpening my memories.

But photographs, and especially old ones, are often difficult to read, to understand. Due to accidents of light and shade and the sometime peculiarities of photographic perspective, they rarely reveal completely the exact forms and structures of objects. Never in the way we experience these with direct human vision. If, however, we have a prior knowledge of such objects, photographs of them can greatly help in their reconstruction. This was the case for me while painting the Joplin mural. Without the photographs I could hardly have made a visual approach to its theme, but without my remembered experiences I could not have developed that.

The Elks' Parade, Joplin, Turn of the Century
Looking South on Main Street from About Third Street

The preceding early photograph of the Elks' Parade on Joplin's Main Street illustrates pretty well how I set about picturing the city in the mural. Most of the buildings shown are now gone, but I knew the street as it was photographically recorded because I saw it everyday from the windows of the newspaper office where I used to work, and walked up and down it when I was through.

In order to make the most use of the photograph, I planned the overall perspective lines of the mural so that they corresponded with those it provided. The only major change I made was to rearrange the lines of the towered Keystone Hotel, the pride of 1906 Joplin, so that I could show its Main Street facade and give a better idea of what the building was really like. This was, however, the only document I could use as I found it, the only one which presented objects with perspectives usable in the mural.

Thomas Hart Benton sketching the towers of the Keystone Hotel
on the scored canvas in his studio, February 1972

Joplin Globe photograph by Joe Sullens

From the "Armstrong" hoist in the right foreground, back through the other mining structures in the rear, all objects had to be reconstructed, their perspectives changed from the photographic records into those of the mural. I had to create substitutes, that is, for what was given by the photographs. I think, however, these are accurate enough to indicate the functions of these objects, which were getting ore out of the ground, first with human power, then horse power, then steam power. Their meanings are reasonably clear.

At this point let us consider the meanings throughout the mural — what they are, or can be, for the people who look at it. In the end, these will be determined largely by what people themselves find in the mural's images. Images necessarily suggest different things to different people, so there can be any number of meanings. For people who have not experienced the things or actions depicted, they will not be the same as for those who have. That makes no difference. Multiple meanings are characteristic of all pictures. It is one of the chief reasons, perhaps, why so many of them, through long periods of time, continue to excite interest.

Now there were, of course, meanings in my own mind which propelled the selection of images and their arrangement in the mural's space. I have just given a clue to what was in my head about the right hand side of the mural when I noted the different kinds of power exercised in Joplin's early mining operations. Moving to mid-center, I was thinking about how Joplin got the most of its early population. Country folks, hearing of the underground treasure there, moved in to get some of it. Some did. Most didn't, but they kept on coming until they turned a small Ozark town into a city.

Although there were lawyers, doctors, engineers and other cultivated people in the Joplin of my time, the language and behavior of the majority of its citizens had a country slant, an Ozark hill flavor. The city was also yet in a horse and buggy, mule and wagon stage. The automobile, though becoming common in the bigger cities of America in 1906, was a rarity in Joplin and probably an impractical one. As I recall the road to my hometown Neosho, no automobile could have gone very far on it without being jolted apart. Anyhow, I have shown no automobiles in the mural. Only the electrically driven street car attests to Joplin's big city status.

In the center foreground, and as a sort of counter play to the poker game to the left, is a symbol of Joplin's religiosity. As with all boom towns, gambling was omnipresent, but the fervors of old time religion found a place there too. Revivals were frequent and enthusiastically attended. They had to be frequent because there were too many temptations offered for backsliding.

Both the revivals and the temptations would have made interesting subjects for the mural, but a much larger space would have been necessary to include them. Besides, the latter might not have been wholly appropriate for a City Hall, even though the City Fathers of boomtime Joplin must certainly have sanctioned them.

I have not wholly ignored this subject, because the "House of Lords" is included in the mural, and that establishment was considerably more than a fancy saloon, or was closely contiguous to something more.

Back of the lamp and the Bible I have, at the request of the mural's sponsors, attempted to represent myself as a young Joplin cartoonist. The likeness is just so so. When I removed the accumulation of wrinkles from my face, nothing much remained.

At the extreme left, the dressed up young lady shows that boomtime Joplin, though assiduously devoted to grosser interests, could aspire to elegance.

These are the meanings that guided my work on the Joplin mural. Some may say they are too simple to be worth the sixty thousand bucks the mural cost. That may be so. But at least they are not phony, which more complicated meanings so often turn out to be. Anyhow, as I said, you can make up your own.

Thomas H. Benton

Thomas Hart Benton in his Kansas City studio, April 1972
KODE-TV photograph by Karl Lee

THOMAS H. BENTON
3616 BELLEVIEW AVENUE
KANSAS CITY, MISSOURI 64111

Jan 18 – '72

Dear Mary Curtis —

You're an energetic researcher and I appreciate the fact. Not often that anybody volunteers to take on my jobs.

However I have found an authentic 1906 afternoon costume for my mural lady or "lady" and have tried it on my model. (She's too skinny for a 1906 girl but I'll pad her out in the proper places) I got it at the K.C. Historical Museum and also found there a 1905 Harper's Bazaar with a lot of accessory details (for my use). So I'm all right on that score — even to shoes and parasol. Just the same keeps advertising for an afternoon (or morning) costume 1905 or 1906. You just might get something better — though I'm appreciating the "moment of decision."

I need either an accurate photo or an accurate diagram of the horse powered hoist ("hist"). I know how it works from my own memory but I need details. See if you can find some old timers who can roughly draw up the proper relations between the power center and the horse. There must be 2 timbers, #1 #2.

or "shaft." One behind the horse, the main one, and one just ahead of him to which his halter is attached. (The photos I have are not at all clear). I have accurate drawings of a sorghum mill but the center of power is much higher than for a mine "hist."

(OVER)

13

I am beginning to get really interested in this picture of 1906 Joplin. You may well get my very best production. I feel at home with it.

The panel, which will be covered with a heavy linen, is now under construction. I'm using an African mahogany for the grid to avoid possibilities of warp. and a composition board (Nova ply type) grooved, glued, screwed down, etc.

Temperature – in room where mural is to be installed should be 45° to 50°, with a "relative" humidity of 50. Tell this to Mr. Cornwell. (It is 50.

My scale drawings are perfect for my purpose. I'll let him know in a week or so, the exact depth of panel.)

Best regards to you & Harry & Rolla. We're moving along pretty good.

Cordially
Tom

Sculpture — 1918
Potter's head — 1945
Celery? — 1965
Trueblood Harvester — '70
contact Forward Poses — '71

P.S. One other small detail.
Does anybody remember whether the Keystone had electric table lamps in 1906. (Bedside table lamps) Or any other hotel? Find out if there were Hotel bedside table lamps in 1906 Joplin. Just find out. I can probably run down their style – probable style.
T

#2. To allay your curiosity "the Gideon Bible" on a table in the foreground just back of the Poker Table. Bibles were omnipresent – the trick is to highlight one of 'em.
T

THE EXECUTION OF THE MURAL

Once he had committed himself to the Joplin mural, Benton worked rapidly. He wrote his sponsors that "hundreds of memory images crowd my mind." These he attributed to his brief return to Joplin in November of 1971, and to "the photographic records you have provided which represent, or suggest, so much of the life I knew there in 1906."

He visited the Joplin Mineral Museum in Schifferdecker Park to reinforce his memory of early mining methods in the area, studying working models, faded photographs, and local minerals from the ground.

His zeal for his new undertaking and his meticulous attention to detail are revealed above in excerpts from a typical letter to the editor during the execution of the mural.

The Keystone Hotel did, indeed, have electric lights in 1906 (as well as Joplin's first elevator), but a retired Methodist minister, whose preacher father had ridden the circuit during that period, recalled rue-fully that only a center fixture with a lone bulb illuminated hotel rooms in Joplin at the turn of the century. He added that although an open Bible usually was on the dresser in the Keystone rooms, there was no special light by which it could be read, and no bedside table. As a result, Benton decided to use a parlor setting for his Bible in the mural, highlighted by a table lamp taken from a mail order catalogue of 1902.

We searched for a genuine revival handbill of early Joplin. Benton remembered seeing such handbills distributed in the district before the frequent revivals in tents and churches. Apparently no copies had been preserved. Therefore, he painted only a corner of a handbill to suggest its presence on the parlor table beside the Bible.

When the canvas was almost completed, the artist telephoned for a loan of sample rocks from the Joplin Mineral Museum. "I want people who know to be able to look at the mural and say, 'By God, that's Joplin, all right. Just look at those minerals.'"

He was so pleased with the native specimens we brought that he arose the next morning at five o'clock to rush out to his studio to begin painting them in the wheel barrow and on the ground of the mining scene. Capturing the irridescence of some of the minerals was a challenge which he attacked with relish.

The touch of geological authenticity was the last work Benton did on the mural. With his brush he signed his name, the date, and the copyright notice in the lower right hand corner.

The following six pages document the development of the mural from the first preliminary sketch to the oil study. Included are old photographs of recognizable influence on the artist's painted concept, and a few working drawings of details for "Joplin at the Turn of the Century."

ROUGH PRELIMINARY DRAWING, 1971
Thematic Concept of "Joplin at the Turn of the Century, 1896-1906"
Pencil, 5¾ x 14⅝"

THE ARTIST'S DRAWING FOR THE ARCHITECT, 1971
Noted for Scale and Horizon Line
Pencil, 7¼ x 22"

WORKING DRAWING FOR THE CARTOON, 1972
Scored to Scale
Pencil, 11 x 28½"

Painted Clay Models in Dioramic Sculpture for the Joplin Mural,
"JOPLIN AT THE TURN OF THE CENTURY, 1896-1906"
1972, Height: 11", Base: 18 x 25"
Preserved by the Artist for the Joplin Exhibition

Oil Study for the Joplin Mural, "JOPLIN AT THE TURN OF THE CENTURY, 1896-1906"
1972, 13¾ x 33½"
Collection of the Artist

OLD PHOTOGRAPHS OF EARLY JOPLIN SCENES

The "Hoist House" at Pinkerton Mine, Number 2

New Prospectors

The Horse Hoister, or "Hoss Hister"

The Old Time Windlass, or "Armstrong" Hoister

JOHN, 1972
Pencil Sketch, 20½ x 13⅞"
Collection of Mr. and Mrs. John Callison,
Kansas City, Missouri

THE MINERS

EARLY MINER AT WORK, 1972
Pencil Sketch, 14½ x 11¼"
Collection of the Artist

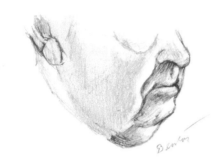

ROLLA, 1972
Pencil Sketch, 4½ x 5½"
Collection of Rolla E. Stephens, Joplin, Missouri

The artist sketching details from life in his Kansas City
studio March 11, 1972.
His model is Joplin realtor Rolla E. Stephens, whose face
appears under a derby in the finished mural.

KODE-TV photograph by Karl Lee

RANDALL, 1972
Pencil Sketch, 13 x 10¾"
Collection of the Artist

THE GAMBLERS

MEL, 1972
Pencil Sketch, 11½ x 14½"
Collection of Mr. and Mrs. Merle E. Welsh,
Prairie Village, Kansas

GENTILITY

KAY, 1972
Pencil Sketch, 5½ x 3¼"
Collection of Mr. and Mrs. John Callison, Kansas City, Missouri

THE PAINTINGS

THIS is the most complete showing of my paintings ever held.

While we were discussing ways and means of putting it together, it was suggested that I write something about each work, telling why I did it and what it meant to me. As this seemed to provide an intimate touch, proper to a homecoming exhibition, I agreed.

However, I couldn't do it. At the first trial, I came up against two insuperable obstacles, my memory and my philosophy. I could remember the experience which occasioned a painting, which put the notion of doing it in my head, but this is only the bare beginning where paintings are concerned. What went on in my mind during the process of painting, what influences bore upon me to determine its form, what reasons for emphasizing one aspect of the motivating experience more than another, turned out to be beyond recollection.

But this was not the real problem. It is possible to make up substitutes for memory failures. The real difficulty arose when I realized that if I were successful in providing the meanings which instigated a picture, I would damage the responses of the people who looked at it, inhibit the creation of their own meanings. This would go too much against what I believe to be the main purpose of art.

I have long ago repudiated the notion, so prevalent in our time, that the purpose of art is to "express" the meanings of the artist. This, it seems to me, is a compensatory notion, an outgrowth of the unhappy fact that art has lost most of its traditional functions in our modern societies. I do not think the artist's meanings are nearly so important as the meanings his creations evoke in their spectators. As a matter of fact, these are the only meanings that count. They are the ones that make for the continuing life of a work of art, spreading its acceptance over generations of men.

It was the growth of such convictions which made me, shortly after the first World War, separate myself from both the "personality exhibitionism" and the "abstract," or, as I see it, purely decorative tendencies of what is called "modern art."

I wanted to use images recognizable enough to evoke human responses in people. Primarily interested in American life, as I was, it was natural that I seek my images there.

But what meanings the paintings have, or come to have, will be the same as those in the mural. You will, in the end, have to find them for yourself.

Thomas H. Benton

RITA AND T. P., 1928
Oil Tempera, 33 x 25''
Collection of Thomas Piacenza Benton

STILL LIFE, 1937
Oil Tempera, 33 x 17"
Collection of Mr. and Mrs. Louis Sosland
Shawnee Mission, Kansas

T. P. AND JAKE, 1938
Oil Tempera, 48 x 31"
Collection of Thomas Piacenza Benton

PERSEPHONE, 1939
Oil Tempera, 71 x 55''
Collection of Rita P. Benton

THE YOUNG FISHERMAN, WHITE RIVER, 1940-60
Oil Tempera, 40 x 38''
Collection of Thomas Piacenza Benton

JESSIE WITH GUITAR, 1956
Oil Tempera, 42½ x 30½''
Collection of Jessie Benton

TRAIL RIDERS, 1964
Acrylic, 56 x 62''
Collection of the Artist

SELF PORTRAIT, 81 YEARS OLD, 1970
Acrylic, 40 x 30''
Collection of Rita P. Benton

SELF PORTRAIT, 19 Years Old, Painted in Paris, France, 1909
Oil, 20¼ x 16¼"
Collection of the Artist

CHESTNUT TREE, CONTRÉ SOLEIL,
Painted in the South of France, 1910
Oil, 20¼ x 16¼"
Collection of the Artist

Sidney Larson uncovered the Benton SELF PORTRAIT, 1909, in the fall of 1966. Recalling the circumstances of his discovery, he writes:

"In recent years, Tom Benton would occasionally call upon me to do some minor conservation on works of art from his earlier days. CHESTNUT TREE, CONTRÉ SOLEIL, 1910, was among them. It had been executed in the Pointillist style of the Post-impressionists, Seurat and Signac. The painting was grey with grime and had not responded to Benton's routine approach to cleaning.

"Back in my studio in Columbia, I removed the top canvas and found a second canvas under the landscape which had been forgotten for sixty years. To the delight of both of us, I determined that it was Benton's self portrait, done in Paris in 1909 when he was 19 years old. It was intense in character and broadly painted. Considering the fact that solvents had soaked through and lain on its surface, the portrait was in relatively good condition.

"Both paintings were subsequently cleaned, lined and revarnished. They contribute an important link in the chain of work from Benton's earliest period."

The Benton family home in Neosho had burned in 1917. These two paintings are all that remain of his Parisian years.

SELF PORTRAIT, 23 Years Old, Painted at Neosho, Missouri, 1912
Oil, 31½ x 22¾''
Collection of Thomas Piacenza Benton

THE EPIC OF AMERICA, Chapter I, 1919-24
DISCOVERY
Oil, 60 x 42"
Collection of the Artist

THE EPIC OF AMERICA

This was a series of related pictures begun in 1919 and worked on through 1926. As originally conceived, the series was to depict, in symbolic fashion, the history of the United States from colonial days to the present. Two sets, each containing five pictures, were exhibited as murals (architectural wall paintings) at the Architectural League in New York City during the early Twenties. Although the project was never completed, it established for me a reputation as a potential muralist, and it was influential in obtaining my mural commissions of the Thirties. This is the first of the series.

T. H. B.

THE EPIC OF AMERICA; Chapter I, 1919-24
PALISADES
Oil, 66 x 72"
Collection of the Artist

THE EPIC OF AMERICA, Chapter I, 1919-24
AGGRESSION
Oil, 66 x 29"
Collection of the Artist

THE EPIC OF AMERICA, Chapter I, 1919-24
PRAYER
Oil, 66 x 72"
Collection of the Artist

THE EPIC OF AMERICA, Chapter I, 1919-24
RETRIBUTION
Oil, 60 x 42"
Collection of the Artist

"The American Historical Epic Series" . . . is "an elaborately programmed, declamatory, and socially conscious history concentrating on a theme that is very much with us today—the white man's conquest of the North American continent and the retribution for his sins." In these paintings, "Mr. Benton first came to a realization of his powers."

(From the article, "Young Artist en Route to the U. S. A.," by John Canaday, art critic for The New York Times, December 10, 1972. Quoted by special permission through the courtesy of Mr. Canaday and The New York Times.)

TIME Magazine's first inside color story appeared Christmas Eve, December 24, 1934. Titled "The U. S. Scene," it featured Thomas Hart Benton's "Self Portrait, Age 36," on the cover in full color.

Reporting a peak season in American art, TIME charted the new trends in taste and subject matter, singling out Thomas Hart Benton as "the most virile of U. S. painters of the U. S. Scene."

Contrasting Benton's realism with the "deliberately unintelligible" work of some of his contemporaries who tried to copy the French with "a profusion of spurious Matisses and Picassos" . . . in a "crazy parade of Cubism, Futurism, Dadaism, Surrealism," TIME commented that Benton painted from "recognizable observations."

The Art section, in its cover story, traced Benton's career from his start in Joplin as a newspaper cartoonist to his 1934 fame as a muralist. It cited in particular the murals in Manhattan's Whitney Museum of American Art, the New School for Social Research, and the latest and best known of that date, the State of Indiana mural, "a huge panorama painted for the Indiana building at the Century of Progress Fair"—the 1933 Chicago World's Fair. It described his murals as peopled with "such typical Americana as revivalists, bootleggers, stevedores, politicians, soda clerks."

According to TIME, "Benton, in his murals and easel paintings, earnestly and almost ferociously strives to record a contemporary history of the U. S. A short wiry man with an unruly crop of black hair, he lives with his beauteous Italian wife and one small son in a picture-cluttered downtown Manhattan flat. To critics who have complained that his murals were loud and disturbing, Artist Benton answers: 'They represent the U. S., which is also loud and not "in good taste." 'I have not found,' he explains, 'the U. S. a standardized mortuary and consequently have no sympathy with that school of detractors whose experience has been limited to first class hotels and the paved highways. At the same time, I am no sentimentalist. I know an ass and the dust of his kicking when I come across it. But I have come across enough of it to be able to discover interesting qualities therein.'

"Thomas Benton has filled scores of notebooks with sketches of the U. S. scene, which eventually find their way into his work. He boasts that all of his burlesque queens, stevedores, Negroes, preachers, and college professors are actual persons. His vivid portraits of them are fast becoming collectors' items and the cost of Bentons has been steadily rising since the Navy put him on the right artistic track. Last week, Thomas Benton, who is usually jolly, had a special reason to be cheerful. He sold his oil, COTTON TOWN" (a color illustration in the article), "to Marshall Field III."

The December 24, 1934 cover of TIME, a weekly newsmagazine, is herein reproduced, with excerpts from its text, by special permission through the courtesy of Time Inc.

SELF PORTRAIT, 36 Years Old, 1925
Oil, 30 x 24″
Collection of Jessie Benton

COTTON LOADING (Red River Landing, Louisiana), 1928
Oil Tempera, 28 x 39"
Collection of the Artist

ENGINEER'S DREAM, 1931
Oil Tempera, 30 x 41 ½"
Collection of the Artist

LORD, HEAL THE CHILD, 1934
Oil Tempera, 46½ x 57½"
Collection of Mr. and Mrs. John Callison
Kansas City, Missouri

"THE SUN TREADER," PORTRAIT OF CARL RUGGLES, 1934
Oil Tempera, 45 x 38"
Collection of The Nelson Gallery-Atkins Museum
Gift of the Friends of Art, 1936
Kansas City, Missouri

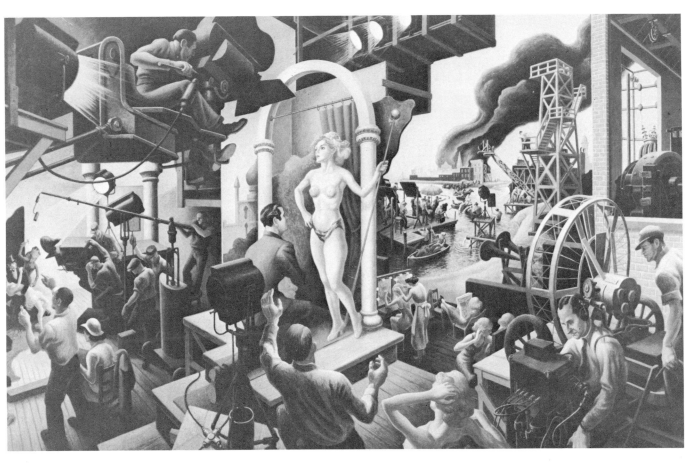

HOLLYWOOD, 1937
Oil Tempera, 55½ x 81"
Collection of the Artist

NEW ENGLAND FARMER HENRY LOOK, 1938
Oil Tempera, 20 x 16"
Collection of Rita P. Benton

FLIGHT OF THE THIELENS (Hurricane at Martha's Vineyard), 1938
Oil Tempera, 26 x 34¾"
Collection of Thomas Piacenza Benton

ROASTING EARS, 1939-40
Oil Tempera, 32 x 39¼"
Collection of the Metropolitan Museum of Art
Arthur H. Hearn Fund, 1939
New York City, New York

DEPARTURE OF THE JOADS, "Grapes of Wrath," 1940
Oil Tempera, 29½ x 45¾"
Collection of the Artist

NEGRO SOLDIER, 1941
Oil Tempera, 58 x 70"
Collection of the State Historical Society of Missouri
Columbia, Missouri

PRELUDE TO DEATH (also, EMBARKATION), 1942
Oil Tempera, 63 x 96"
Collection of the Artist

PORTRAIT OF A MUSICIAN, 1949
Oil Tempera, 48 1/2 x 32''
Collection of the Museum of Art and Archeology
Columbia, Missouri

COUNTY POLITICS, mid '50s
Oil Tempera, 20¾ x 26½"
Collection of Rita P. Benton

PORTRAIT OF CARL SANDBURG, 1956
Oil Tempera, 31⅜ x 21¼"
Collection of Rita P. Benton

STUDY FOR THE TRUMAN MURAL, "INDEPENDENCE AND THE OPENING OF THE WEST"
1959-60
Acrylic, 30 x 42"
Collection of the Artist

TRIAL BY JURY (also, DAMAGE SUIT), 1964
Oil, 30 x 40"
Collection of the Artist

THE TWIST DANCERS, 1964
Acrylic, 32 x 55½"
Collection of the Artist

JESSIE AND ANTHONY, 1965
Acrylic, 24 x 30"
Collection of Anthony Benton Gude

TEN POUND HAMMERS, 1965-66
Acrylic, 30 x 23½"
Collection of Mr. and Mrs. Robert E. Stroud
Shawnee Mission, Kansas

FISHERMEN'S CAMP, BUFFALO RIVER, 1968
Oil Tempera, 30 x 38''
Collection of Mr. and Mrs. Robert E. Stroud
Shawnee Mission, Kansas

MISSOURI LAWYER, 1969
Acrylic, 18 x 24"
Collection of the Artist

THE RACE (On Menemsha Pond, Martha's Vineyard), 1971
Oil, 28 x 36"
Collection of Rita P. Benton

THE GLORIOUS WHITEWASHER, 1939
Illustration for The Limited Editions Club
"Adventures of Tom Sawyer"
Pen and Ink, 9 x 6"
Collection of the State Historical Society of Missouri
Columbia, Missouri

"DOAN' YOU 'MEMBER . . .," 1942
Illustration for The Limited Editions Club
"Adventures of Huckleberry Finn"
Sepia, Pen and Ink, 9¾ x 6½"
Collection of the State Historical Society of Missouri
Columbia, Missouri

LIFE ON THE MISSISSIPPI, 1944
Frontispiece for The Limited Editions Club
"Life on the Mississippi"
Watercolor, Pen and Ink, 10⅛ x 6¾"
Collection of the State Historical Society of Missouri
Columbia, Missouri

BENTON'S MARK TWAIN

The largest and most comprehensive retrospective exhibition of Thomas Hart Benton's works to date is assembled in the gallery of the Spiva Art Center March 24 through April 27. All illustrations in this book are from the exhibit or pertain to the mural and its execution. However, because support of Benton's art as an opening feature of the Centennial is city-wide, this page is devoted to the mention of additional aspects of his work which are on display in four Joplin banks and in the administration building of the Joplin R-8 Public School System.

The illustrations to the left suggest Benton's natural affinity with his fellow Missourian, Mark Twain, in three books published by The Limited Editions Club. A generous number of Benton's original drawings for the Mark Twain classics is on loan by the State Historical Society of Missouri at Columbia, which owns the entire series.

Convinced that the function of an illustrator is to stimulate the reader's imagination and not to stifle it with over-realistic pictures, Benton kept his drawings light and spare. Nevertheless, he admitted to "a big, slambang emotional indulgence" in his Mark Twain assignments, journeying with knapsack and sketch pad into the back country, along creek banks and on river packets down the Mississippi to recapture the scenes of Tom Sawyer and Huck Finn—and thereby those of his own boyhood.

Examples of Benton's pen and ink drawings for "The Adventures of Tom Sawyer," the earliest of this series, may be seen downtown at the First National Bank and Trust Company of Joplin and at its affiliate at the Northpark Mall, the Community National Bank of Joplin.

Illustrations from "The Adventures of Huckleberry Finn," which Benton has reread annually throughout his life as "escape literature," are at the United Missouri Bank of Joplin. The artist incorporated sepia wash in the Huckleberry Finn drawings.

To the basic pen and ink drawings for "Life on the Mississippi," Benton added sepia wash in some instances, watercolor in others, to reflect the character of the river and its people. The Commerce Bank of Joplin has mounted a display of them in its lobby.

In 1955 Benton completed a uniquely designed mural for Lincoln University at Jefferson City, Missouri, which, until recently, has been on view in Page Library on the campus. Presently it is on loan by the university to the First National Bank and Trust Company of Joplin in honor of the Centennial.

The mural, which is eight and a half feet tall by six feet wide, portrays Abraham Lincoln as the central figure which, in Benton's words, is "symbolic of universal freedom from all bondage, from all tyranny, from all injustice, . . . a freedom that cannot be maintained without knowledge." He studied numerous photographs of Lincoln before arriving finally at the painted concept which "has no existence in record," but is "an imaginary composite of ideas and intuitions." (From the dedication speech by Thomas Hart Benton at Lincoln University, May 15, 1955.)

A traveling educational exhibit of sixty Benton drawings in reproduction from the Missouri State Council on the Arts is housed in the administration building of the Joplin public schools. Among its subjects are scenes and landscapes from Missouri, some studies for Benton murals, and assorted genre scenes that depict other areas of the United States. It constitutes another expression of the focus on Thomas Hart Benton at the opening of the Joplin Centennial.

THE SCULPTURES

RITA, 1918
Bronze, Height: 14½", Base: 11¼ x 19½"
Collection of Rita P. Benton

CASEY (also, CASY, "Grapes of Wrath"), mid '40s
Bronze, Height: 5½", Base: 3x3½"
Collection of Jessie Benton

TEN POUND HAMMER ("John Henry"), 1965
Bronze, Height: 10½", Base: 11x9"
Collection of Thomas Piacenza Benton

CONTACT, 1971
 Bronze, Height: 8¼'', Base 9x18''
Collection of Jessie Benton

FORWARD PASS, 1971
 Bronze, Height: 10½'', Base: 12x25¼''
Collection of Thomas Piacenza Benton

TRUMPET VINE, 1938
Pencil, Pen and Ink and Wash, 14 x 13"
Collection of Rita P. Benton

THE DRAWINGS

MR. PRESIDENT, 1971
Head Study for THE OLD PRESIDENT, HARRY S. TRUMAN AT 86
Pencil, 8¾ x 7"
Collection of the Artist

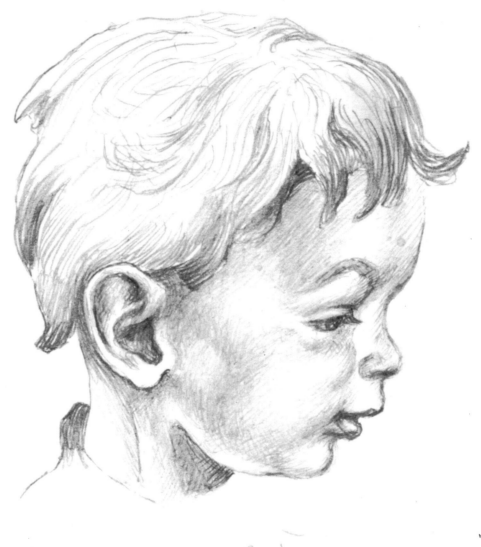

ANTHONY, 1965
Head Study for JESSIE AND ANTHONY
Pencil, 4½ x 3¾"
Collection of Anthony Benton Gude

JESSIE, 1965
Head Study for JESSIE AND ANTHONY
Pencil, 8 x 5½″
Collection of Jessie Benton

CLAY ROGERS, 1969
Study for MISSOURI LAWYER
Pencil, 8½ x 7″
Collection of the Artist

CARL RUGGLES, 1934
Study for "THE SUN TREADER," PORTRAIT OF CARL RUGGLES
Pencil, 8½ x 7"
Collection of Rita P. Benton

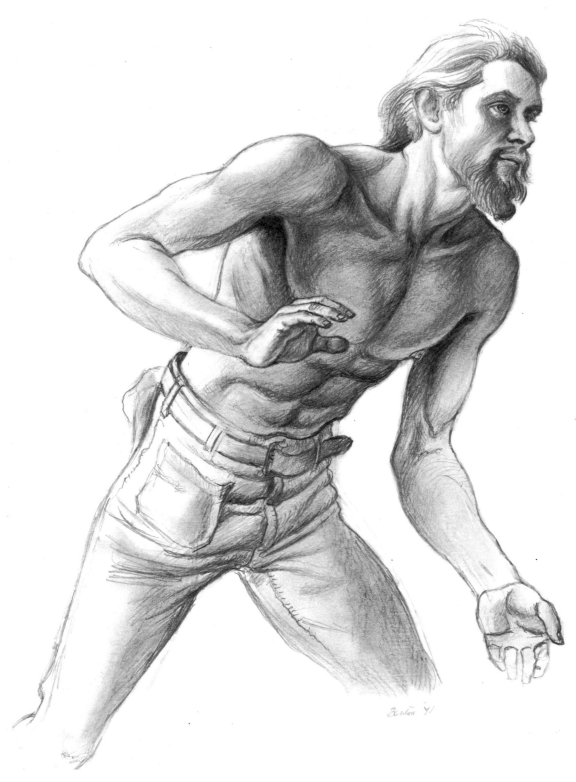

EDDIE, 1971
Study for "POTIPHAR'S WIFE"
Pencil, 15 x 10"
Collection of Eddie Samoa, Boston, Massachusetts

MISSOURI OAK TREE, Mid '30s
Study for PERSEPHONE
Pencil, Pen and Ink and Wash, 17 x 10¾"
Collection of Mr. and Mrs. Henry Warten, Joplin, Missouri

Studies for PERSEPHONE, 1938-39
Pencil, 18 x 10½''
Collection of Rita P. Benton

Studies for PERSEPHONE, 1938-39
Pencil, 7½ x 6½'' and 17 x 11''
Collection of Rita P. Benton

COUNTRY MUSICIANS, 1938 ·
Pencil, Pen and Ink and Wash, 14 x 14½"
Collection of the Artist

OZARK HUNTER, 1924
Pencil, 14 x 8½"
Collection of the Artist

COUNTY COURTHOUSE, Mid '50s
Study for COUNTY POLITICS
Pencil, Pen and Ink and Wash, 12 x 15½"
Collection of Rita P. Benton

SATURDAY DISCUSSION, Late '30s
Pencil, Pen and Ink and Wash, 8½ x 11"
Collection of Mr. and Mrs. William F. Navran, Shawnee Mission, Kansas

CHURCH OF CONCORDIA, MISSOURI, 1950
Pencil, 10¾ x 16"
Collection of the Artist

COUNTRY TOWN, 1938
Pencil, 10½ x 17"
Collection of the Artist

BUFFALO RIVER, 1969
Pencil, Pen and Ink and Wash, 8⅞ x 12¼"
Collection of the Artist

UPPER MISSOURI RIVER, 1965
Study for LEWIS AND CLARK AT EAGLE CREEK
Pencil, Pen and Ink and Wash, 10¾ x 13½"
Collection of the Artist

OLD MAC AT THE BUGGY, or FRANK'S BUGGY, 1969
Pencil, Pen and Ink and Wash, 11½ x 17⅝"
Collection of the Artist

FLOODTIME IN THE BOOT HEEL, MISSOURI, 1937
Pencil, Pen and Ink and Wash, 8¼ x 11¾"
Collection of the Artist

MOUNTED COWBOY, 1952, 8½ x 6½"
Frontispiece for The Limited Editions Club
"Green Grow the Lilacs"
Collection of the State Historical Society of Missouri
Columbia, Missouri

THE LITHOGRAPHS

The eighty-two lithographs on exhibit at the Spiva Art Center, which are listed here, are from the collection of the State Historical Society of Missouri, Columbia.

Two rare lithograph stones from the State Historical Society also are on display, made by Benton for offset illustrations of The Limited Editions Club book, "Green Grow the Lilacs," by Lynn Riggs —the source play for the musical stage classic, "Oklahoma!"

Crayon drawings on both sides of one stone are:

Frontispiece, MOUNTED COWBOY DRIVING CATTLE

AUNT ELLER MURPHY, CHURN-ING

LAUREY

CURLY FIRING PISTOL BEHIND JEETER

Crayon drawings on both sides of the other stone are:

OLD MAN PECK AND GUITAR AT SQUARE DANCE

CURLY AND LAUREY, WINDMILL BACKGROUND

SHIVAREE WITH LAUREY AND CURLY ON HAYSTACK

AT THE DOOR, AUNT ELLER CONFRONTS THE DEPUTY AND CROWD

CURLY FIRING PISTOL BEHIND JEETER
Lithograph Illustration for "Green Grow the Lilacs"
Limited Editions Club Book
1952, 8 ½ x 6½"
Collection of the State Historical Society of Missouri
Columbia, Missouri

THE STATION, also TRAIN IN THE STATION,
OKLAHOMA, EDGE OF THE PLAINS
1929, Edition of 50
5⅞ x 6⅛"

COMING 'ROUND THE MOUNTAIN, also MISSOURI MUSICIANS,
SHE'LL BE DRIVING SIX WHITE HORSES, OZARK MUSICIANS
1931, Edition of 75
11⅛ x 8⅜"

GOING WEST, also EXPRESS TRAIN
1934, Edition of 75
11½ x 22½"

MINSTREL SHOW
1934, Edition of 100
9 x 11⅝"

PLOWING IT UNDER, also PLOWING
1934, Edition of 250
8 x 13⅜"

WAITING FOR THE REVOLUTION
1934, Edition of 10
4 x 7½"

MISSOURI FARMYARD, also OZARK FARMYARD,
KANSAS FARMYARD
From The Missouri State Capitol Mural Series
1936, Edition of 250
10⅛ x 16"

FRANKIE AND JOHNNIE
From The Missouri State Capitol Mural Series
1936, Edition of 100
16⅜ x 22⅛"

HUCK FINN
From The Missouri State Capitol Mural Series
1936, Edition of 100
16¼ x 21⅝"

JESSE JAMES
From The Missouri State Capitol Mural Series
1936, Edition of 100
16⅜ x 22⅛"

GOIN' HOME
1937, Edition of 250
9⅜ x 12"

A DRINK OF WATER
1937, Edition of 250
10 x 14¼"

FLOOD (Missouri Boot Heel)
1937, Edition of 196
9¼ x 12¼"

INVESTIGATION (Missouri Boot Heel)
1937, Edition of 193
9⅜ x 12⅝"

LONESOME ROAD
1938, Edition of 250
9¾ x 12½"

I GOTTA GAL ON SOURWOOD MOUNTAIN
1938, Edition of 250
12½ x 9⅛"

HOMESTEAD, also IN THE OZARKS
1938, Edition of 250
9 x 13⅛"

HAYSTACK
1938, Edition of 250
10⅜ x 12⅞"

EDGE OF TOWN
1938, Edition of 250
9 x 10¾"

RAINY DAY
1938, Edition of 250
8¾ x 13⅜"

THE POET
1938, Edition of 75
8⅞ x 12⅜"

NOON, also APPROACHING STORM
1938, Edition of 200
9¾ x 12⅞"

SUNDAY MORNING
1939, Edition of 250
9⅝ x 12⅜"

CRADLING WHEAT
1939, Edition of 250
9¾ x 12"

PLANTING, also SPRING PLOWING
1939, Edition of 250
10 x 12½"

PRODIGAL SON
1939, Edition of 250
10 x 13¼"

FRISKY DAY
1939, Edition of 250
7¾ x 12"

THE WOODPILE, also WOOD CUTTER
1939, Edition of 250
8¾ x 10⅞"

SHALLOW CREEK
1939, Edition of 250
14¼ x 9¼"

DOWN THE RIVER, also THE YOUNG FISHERMAN
1939, Edition of 250
12½ x 10"

DEPARTURE OF THE JOADS
From "The Grapes of Wrath" Series
1939, Edition of 100
12¾ x 18¼"

MA JOAD
From "The Grapes of Wrath" Series
1939, Edition of 25
6¾ x 6¾"

PA JOAD
From "The Grapes of Wrath" Series
1939, Edition of 25
9½ x 7"

SHARON JOAD
From "The Grapes of Wrath" Series
1939, Edition of 25
7½ x 6"

TOM JOAD
From "The Grapes of Wrath" Series
1939, Edition of 25
9½ x 6¾"

CASY, also THE REVEREND JIM CASY
From "The Grapes of Wrath" Series
1939, Edition of 25
8¼ x 4½"

HOEING COTTON
(A Trial Print)
1940, Edition of 10
9⅝ x 12½"

THE FENCE MENDER
1940, Edition of 250
10 x 14"

INSTRUCTION
1940, Edition of 250
10½ x 12¼"

AARON
1941, Edition of 250
12⅞ x 9½"

SUNSET
1941, Edition of 204
10 x 13⅛"

OLD MAN READING
1941, Edition of 250
10 x 12⅛"

ARKANSAS EVENING, also NEBRASKA EVENING
1941, Edition of 250
10 x 13"

SLOW TRAIN THROUGH ARKANSAS
1941, Edition of 250
10 x 12¾"

THE MEETING
1941, Edition of 250
8⅞ x 11½"

THRESHING
1941, Edition of 250
9¼ x 14"

SWAMPLAND, also THE SWAMP
From "Swamp Water" Series
1941, Edition of 100
17¾ x 12¾"

MAN AND DOG, also THE HUNTER, BEN RAGAN AND TROUBLE
From "Swamp Water" Series
1941, Edition of 100
11 x 7¼"

MAN, also TOM KEEFER
From "Swamp Water" Series
1941, Edition of 100
9 x 7½"

JESSIE AND JAKE
1942, Edition of 250
13⅜ x 9⅞"

THE RACE, also HOMEWARD BOUND
1942, Edition of 250
10 x 13¼"

NIGHT FIRING, also TOBACCO FIRING
1943, Edition of 250
8¾ x 13⅛"

MORNING TRAIN, also SOLDIER'S FAREWELL
1943, Edition of 250
9⅜ x 13½"

LETTER FROM OVERSEAS
1943, Edition of 250
9⅝ x 13⅛"

THE MUSIC LESSON
1943, Edition of 250
10⅛ x 12½"

SPRING TRYOUT
1943, Edition of 250
9½ x 13⅝"

THE FARMER'S DAUGHTER
1944, Edition of 250
9⅞ x 13⅛"

WRECK OF THE OL' 97
1944, Edition of 250
10¼ x 15"

FIRE IN THE BARNYARD
1944, Edition of 250
8¾ x 13⅜"

LOADING CORN, also SHUCKING CORN
1945, Edition of 250
10¼ x 13¼"

BACK FROM THE FIELDS
1945, Edition of 250
9¼ x 12⅞"

WHITE CALF
1945, Edition of 250
10¾ x 13¼"

ISLAND HAY
1945, Edition of 250
10 x 12⅝"

GATESIDE CONVERSATION
1946, Edition of 250
9⅞ x 14"

AFTER THE BLOW
1946, Edition of 250
9¾ x 13⅞"

THE CORRAL
1948, Edition of 250
9⅜ x 13⅝"

THE BOY
1948, Edition of 250
9½ x 13¾"

PRAYER MEETING, also WEDNESDAY EVENING
1949, Edition of 300
9 x 12¼"

THE HYMN SINGER, also THE MINSTREL, BURL IVES
1950, Edition of 500
16 x 12⅜"

PHOTOGRAPHING THE BULL
1950, Edition of 500
12 x 16"

NEW ENGLAND FARM
1951, Edition of 300
9 x 14"

HOMECOMING—KAW VALLEY
1951, Special Offset Edition for the Congress of the United States
Cover Picture for New Republic, "Disaster on the Kaw"
11½ x 14½"

WEST TEXAS
1952, Edition of 300
11 x 13⅞"

RUNNING HORSES
1955, Edition of 100
12½ x 16½"

TEN POUND HAMMER ("John Henry")
1967, Edition of 300
13¾ x 9¾"

THE LITTLE FISHERMAN
1967, Edition of 300
14⅛ x 10"

SORGHUM MILL
1968, Edition of 250
9⅝ x 13¾"

JOE'S PLACE, also DISCUSSION
1968, Edition of 250
9¾ x 12"

SELF PORTRAIT, 81 YEARS OLD
1971, Edition of 300
19½ x 13¾"

FORWARD PASS
1971, Edition of 200
12⅞ x 19¾"

ACKNOWLEDGMENTS

This book could not have been possible without the faith
and backing of the hundreds of contributors to the Joplin Council
for the Arts-Benton Fund, and the leadership of the executive board
of the Joplin Council for the Arts.

The board of directors of the Spiva Art Center, with Mrs. Duane
Hunt, president, and Darral A. Dishman, director, collaborated
importantly; as did Leon R. Kassab, president of the Joplin '73
Centennial Association and his board of directors.

Others to whom special credit is due in connection with the book are:

Ross E. Taggart, senior curator of the Nelson Gallery-Atkins
Museum at Kansas City, whose advice and suggestions about the costs
and planning of a catalogue were particularly helpful at the
inception of our project.

Sidney Larson, consultant for the exhibition, whose expertise in
the organization of a major exhibit provided immediate assistance
whenever a special need arose, and whose knowledge of art in general
and Thomas Hart Benton in particular bolstered our efforts in two
years of preparation.

William F. Navran, first vice president of Burd & Fletcher Company,
who burst upon us the idea of going hard-bound, and encouraged
us in other embellishments.

Mrs. Addison E. McMechan, who patiently read proof and braved a
bitter winter on our adjoining country road to do so.

Miss Margaret Hager, chief librarian of the Joplin Public Library,
who read final proof.

Mrs. Milton W. Brietzke, who, with Mrs. McMechan and Mrs. Tom
Dilworth, assisted in the publicity and promotion of the book.

Mrs. Milo Johnson, whose professional experience and meticulous
keeping of records made her an invaluable chairman of book sales.

Mrs. Robert Raudenbush, Mrs. Polly Thompson White, Mrs. Hal
Patterson and Mrs. Douglas Day, who helped in the compilation of
mailing lists and in sales and shipping arrangements.

Bob Phillips, Joplin television writer-producer, and Karl Lee,
photographer, whose one-hour documentary, "THOMAS HART
BENTON: THE LAST MURAL," for KODE-TV and the Gilmore
Broadcasting Corporation, furnished reels of photographic studies
of Benton in action.

And, above all, Henry Warten, whose ideas, support and legal
guidance, as well as his uncomplaining expenditure of time and
energy, have made him a full partner in this undertaking.

For sources of information, we are indebted mainly to Benton's autobiographical books, "An Artist in America," now in its third revised edition by the University of Missouri Press, 1968; and "An American in Art," published by the University Press of Kansas, 1969.

"A Note by the Illustrator," by Thomas Hart Benton for the Limited Editions Club's "Huckleberry Finn," 1942, gave insights into his style and his approach to illustrating a narrative.

"The Lithographs of Thomas Hart Benton," compiled and edited by Creekmore Fath, University of Texas Press, 1969, was helpful in cataloguing the lithographs.

Our chief authorities in the entire enterprise were Tom and Rita Benton, whose genuine interest and active participation in our efforts have attained for Joplin the seemingly unattainable—a Thomas Hart Benton mural, the largest retrospective exhibition to date of Benton works, and a book to commemorate the two in honor of the city's Centennial.

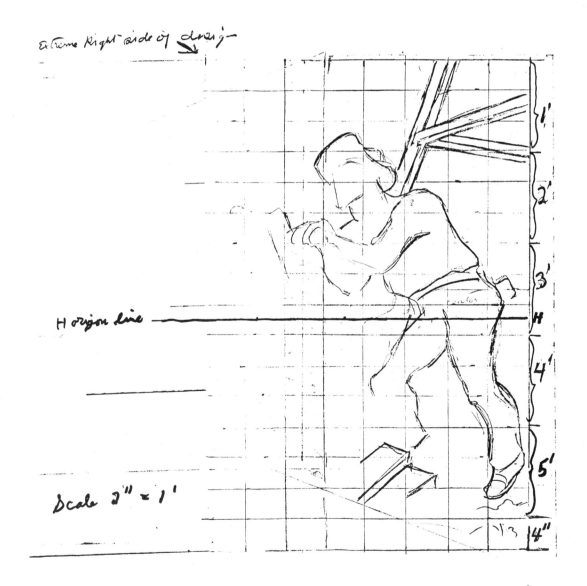